Me and My Friends

# I Can Be a Friend

written by Daniel Nunn

illustrated by Clare Elsom

Raintree is an imprint of Capstone Global Library Limited,
a company incorporated in England and Wales having
its registered office at 7 Pilgrim Street, London, EC4V 6LB –
Registered company number: 6695582

www.raintreepublishers.co.uk
myorders@raintreepublishers.co.uk

Edited by Brynn Baker
Designed by Steve Mead and Kyle Grenz
Production by Helen McCreath
Original illustrations © Clare Elsom
Originated by Capstone Global Library Ltd
Printed and bound in Spain by Grafos S.A.

ISBN 978 1 406 28161 3
18 17 16 15 14
10 9 8 7 6 5 4 3 2 1

**British Library Cataloguing in Publication Data**
A full catalogue record for this book is available from
the British Library.

# Contents

# Being a friend

I share with my friend.

Good friends share.

I take turns with my friend.

Good friends take turns.

I tell the truth to my friend.

Good friends tell the truth.

I listen to my friend.

Good friends listen.

I care for my friend.

Good friends care.

I help my friend.

Good friends help.

I play nicely with my friends.

Good friends play nicely.

I have fun with my friends!

Good friends have fun!

# Being friendly quiz

Which of these pictures shows being friendly?

Did being friendly make these children happy? Why?
Do you like being friendly?

# Picture glossary

**care**  to look after your friends and help them to be happy

**friend**  person you care about and have fun with

**share**  to divide something up between you and your friends or take turns using it

# Index

# Notes for teachers and parents

**BEFORE READING**
**Building background:** Ask children to describe what makes a good friend.
How do they make friends? What's the best thing about having a friend?

**AFTER READING**
**Recall and reflection:** Ask the class how children in the book had fun. What things
do they like to do? (Playing a game, jumping a rope.) Do the children in the
book look happy? How can they tell?

**Sentence knowledge:** Choose a page, and ask children to identify a capital letter
and a full stop. Why is there a capital letter? What does a full stop signal?

**Word knowledge (phonics):** Ask children to point to the word *with* on page 4.
Sound out the three phonemes in the word *w/ i/ th*. Ask children to sound out
each phoneme as they point at the letters, and then blend the sounds together
to make the word *with*. Ask them which of these words have the same sound in
the middle: *pin, pan, bit, but, ten* or *tin*.

**Word recognition:** Look at the word *nicely* on page 17. Help children to clearly
hear the two syllables (*nice/ ly*). Say the word slowly while clapping once for
each syllable.

**AFTER-READING ACTIVITIES**
Ask children to work with partners to draw a picture of something they like to do
with good friends. They can write a sentence or dictate a sentence about the
picture. Bind the pages into a class book about friendship.

# In this book

**Topic**
friendship

**Topic words and phrases**
care
friends
have fun
help
play
share
take turns
tell the truth

**Sentence stems**
I ___ for my friend.
I ___ to my friend.
I ___with my friend.
Good friends ___.

**High-frequency words**
for
have
I
my
the
to
with